Sharon McKay & David MacLeod

TAKE A HIKE

cover by
SAM SISCO

chapter illustrations by
SUSAN GARDOS

vignettes
YÜKSEL HASSAN

SCHOLASTIC INC.
New York Toronto London Auckland Sydney

ISBN 0-590-80841-9

Text copyright © 1995 by Sharon McKay and David MacLeod. Illustrations copyright © 1995 by Scholastic Canada Ltd. All rights reserved. Published by Scholastic Inc., 555 Broadway, New York, NY 10012, by arrangement with Scholastic Canada Ltd.

12 11 10 9 8 7 6 5 4 3 2 1   6 7 8 9/9 0 1/0

Printed in the U.S.A.   23

First Scholastic printing, April 1996

*To Ian McKay, who plans to hike
the highlands of Scotland in a small car.*

*And to Angus MacLeod,
who blazed many a trail through uncharted forests
in search of the perfect Christmas tree.*

Our thanks to:

Allan Foster, curator and naturalist at the Kortright Centre for Conservation, Kleinberg;

Bill Savage, backpacker and former environmental educator with the London Board of Education;

Valerie Wilkins, Poison Control, Hospital for Sick Children, Toronto, Ontario;

Philippa Campsie, urban planner and urban hiker;

Rosemary Toth, editor, who edited beyond the call of duty;

Diane Kerner, senior editor and friend;

Don Sedgwick, Scholastic's in-house bird guy;

and Susan Gardos, Andrea Casault and art director Yüksel Hassan.

TABLE OF CONTENTS

STARTING OUT

COUNT DOWN
EQUIPMENT
FIRST AID
FINDING YOUR WAY
WEATHER
BUG ATTACK

TO THE READER

Dear Reader,

You're going to love hiking. It's fun, inexpensive, and it can be done just about anywhere, at any time of year. You can go out for half an hour, or make a whole day of it.

Some tips on how to use this book:

Flip through the Table of Contents and check out all the hiking possibilities. This is a handbook, so you don't have to read the whole book in order. Try trekking through it this way:

- read the section on the type of hike you are planning: city, beach, forest, etc.
- make sure you have read the entire Starting Out section before you set out. It's full of vital hiking information, no matter where you're planning to go.
- then, check the Looking at Nature section for your particular interests: rocks, trees, wildlife and so on.

Bring this book along with you, especially if you're going to be doing any of the Science in a Backpack activities.

Housebound? Well, there are still lots of things to do. Look for the Rainy Day Activities everywhere in the book. These are great for trying out at home. They're marked with this symbol:

And check the Armchair Hiker section at the end for knot-tying instructions and fun quizzes.

So take a hike, enjoy, have fun and stay safe.

Happy trails,

Sharon and David

2

COUNT DOWN

Before you set off on your hike, there are some things you should be aware of. Here's a checklist to see if you're ready. If you answer "no" to **any** of the following, you need more preparation. If you answer "yes," you're ready for some fun!

Are you in good shape?

☐ YES   ☐ NO

One way to prepare yourself for a long hike is by walking everywhere — to the store, to school and up stairs (no elevators or escalators) before you make serious tracks.

Do you know where you're going on your hike — the exact route and how long it will take?

☐ YES   ☐ NO

Remember, you must gear the pace to the slowest member of your group.

Does a responsible adult know and approve of your plans, the route and expected return time?

☐ YES   ☐ NO

Someone must know where to look for you if necessary.

Have you discussed a lost and found plan with your hiking partners? (See pages 23–26.)

☐ YES   ☐ NO

If you have a medical condition such as asthma, diabetes or severe allergies, is there a member of your hiking team who knows how to handle an emergency?

☐ YES   ☐ NO

Do you have the right equipment? (See pages 5–9.)

☐ YES   ☐ NO

Do you know the weather forecast?

☐ YES   ☐ NO

NEVER HIKE ALONE!

Go with a group — four or five is ideal. Always get permission and tell an adult the route you plan to take. If you can get an adult to go with you, that's even better.

Equipment

Notebook

A nature notebook is a must for hikers. Any blank, pocket-sized book will do. It can also double as a temporary flower press or spider web collector.

You can also use *this* book to make notes. Bring it along to flip through while you're on the trail.

As you discover a type of tree, bird, flower, plant or building, make notes in the margins and carry on. Then maybe one day, years and years from now, you'll find your book again and remember . . .

Remember that whatever you take on a hike must return with you. Hikers want to see nature, not litter.

A Word about Backpacks

If you already have a backpack, or can borrow one, great! If you're thinking of buying a backpack, look for one made of a durable nylon material. It should have well padded and easily adjustable shoulder straps and a padded waist strap. (Compartments for carrying stuff are also useful.)

The most important thing is that the pack is comfortable on your back when it's full. So before you choose your pack, fill it up, strap it on and take a stroll around. Will it be comfortable on your back for a whole day lugging gear? If not, keep looking.

For regular day-hikes you won't need a backpack with a frame. But if you plan to tote a lot of stuff, keep this rule in mind — your full pack shouldn't weigh more than one quarter of your weight. Heavy items should go at the bottom of your pack to keep the weight on your hips. Lighter items, a jacket or blanket for instance, go on top.

If you are carrying a backpack and crossing a stream, unbuckle the waist strap. Otherwise, if you fall forward in the stream the pack could pin you under the water.

What to Carry in Your Backpack

- [ ] a map and compass
- [ ] sunglasses
- [ ] sunscreen
- [ ] a pocketknife (if you have one)
- [ ] chalk (to mark trees if you go off the path)
- [ ] a first-aid kit (see page 16)
- [ ] a space blanket — a silvery, lightweight sheet
- [ ] insect repellent
- [ ] money (change for a pay phone)
- [ ] a couple of small plastic bags (for garbage or to wrap your feet in)
- [ ] a rain jacket with hood and pants (if the weather is likely to turn bad)
- [ ] a windbreaker
- [ ] a sweater
- [ ] extra socks

- [ ] a notebook
- [ ] a pencil
- [ ] toilet paper
- [ ] a water bottle
- [ ] snacks
- [ ] a flashlight
- [ ] a small unbreakable mirror
- [ ] a piece of strong, light rope about 3 to 3.5 meters long

Other Necessities

Carry a whistle. You may want to attach it to your belt or carry it on a string around your neck. A loud, store-bought whistle is best. After all, a blow on a whistle not only alerts other hikers if you are lost or falling behind but it can also scare off animals.

Carry some identification in your pocket. And speaking of pockets, use them to the max. Then if you lose your backpack you'll still have a few things to carry you through. And, of course, at least one member of your party should have a watch.

Decide on the science experiments that you'd like to do on your hike and make sure you bring along the necessary equipment.

Extras

☐ a magnifying glass

☐ a shatter-proof container with a lid, such as a yogurt container or plastic peanut-butter jar

☐ a small shovel or big spoon

☐ a leaf or flower press

☐ binoculars

☐ a camera

☐ string and some rubber bands

Water, Water Everywhere but Not a Drop to Drink

Do not drink the water from streams or lakes. Just because the water looks clear does not mean it is safe to drink.

It's really important to replace the sweat you lose, especially when hiking in warm weather. Be sure to bring enough water or thirst-quenching beverage (not pop) with you. Carry a water bottle on your belt and an extra supply in your pack.

Did you know that an average-sized person can sweat 13 liters of water a day?

HIKING STAFF

There are many uses for a hiking stick or staff. Here are just some:

- It can take some of the weight off your feet on long hikes.
- It can help you keep your balance on rough or slippery terrain.
- It can help you to hop over small streams or ditches.
- It can measure the depth of water or snow.
- It can become a fishing pole.
- It can be used to help reach someone in trouble if soft ground or ice prevents you from getting close enough.
- It can be used to hold up a lean-to or a pot.
- It can be used to protect yourself against unfriendly animals.

Keep your eyes peeled for a good stick. You might be able to find a fallen branch or you could discover a staff that another hiker has left behind for you (some hikers call treasures like this "trail booty"!).

Make Your Own Hiking Staff

You will need:

☐ a pocketknife

☐ a fallen branch or stem (the straighter the better).
The staff should be 3 to 4 cm thick and about the
same height as the hiker.

- Remove all of the bark from the branch with the knife. Try
  to get right down to the smooth wood. This will make the
  staff more comfortable to hold.

If you want to make your staff even more interesting,
get an adult to help you do any or all of the following:

- With your pocketknife, carve a groove about 2.5 cm wide
  and 3 mm deep into the staff a little ways up from the
  bottom. Wrap some fishing line into the groove around the
  staff. Have an adult carve or drill a tiny hole into the staff
  near the fishing line. Stick the barbed end of a fish-hook
  into this hole. Your staff now has a built-in fishing rod!
- Take a ruler and pencil and, starting at the bottom of the
  staff, make the following marks: mark from 1-10
  centimeters, then mark every 5 centimeters until you get to
  30. After 30 centimeters, mark in 15-centimeter intervals
  until you get to the top. You can mark the other side of the
  staff in inches. Cut grooves into the staff where you have
  marked with pencil. Make the grooves deep enough so that
  they can be easily seen and won't wear off. Now you can
  measure things you find on your hike.
- You might also want to carve your own mark or design into
  your staff to give it that personal touch.

Let's not forget about knife safety!
Always cut away from yourself and keep
the hand holding the object being cut
behind the direction of the knife.
Keep the knife closed when not in use.

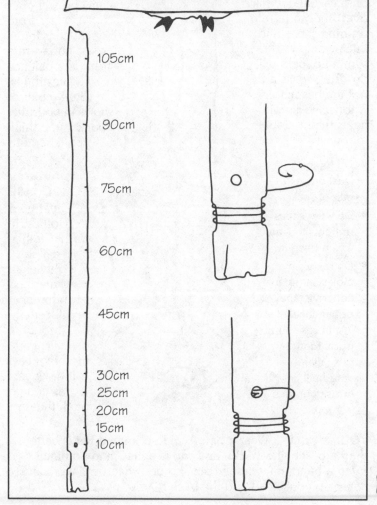

105cm

90cm

75cm

60cm

45cm

30cm
25cm
20cm
15cm
10cm

Wear It

It's best to wear very bright clothes when hiking. Tell your friends to do the same.

Feet First

Start from the bottom up. Hiking boots are fine, but on a casual day-hike over smooth terrain, running shoes and thick wool or synthetic socks will do. Tube socks are not the best choice. Choose socks with heels that fit your foot well.

- Do bring at least one extra pair of socks.

- Do wear shoes or boots that are well broken-in.

- Do carry moleskin (fuzzy adhesive tape) or bandages just in case your trusty footwear rubs against your heel or hurts your toes.

Bottoms Up

You'll probably want to wear long pants. They will protect your legs from scratches in tall grass and form a front-line defence against bugs. (Stuff a pair of shorts in your day pack if you think you'll be hot.)

Top Half

Layer your clothes. In warm weather, a T-shirt, lightweight sweater and windbreaker will get you through a chilly early morning. Peel off the layers as you go through the day.

Your Head   Wear a hat. A wide-brimmed hat is better than a baseball cap. But any cap is better than nothing! Even a bandana wrapped around your head will work. Just cover up your head and the back of your neck.

Hat Experiment

We've all heard this before: "Don't forget to put on your hat." Why is a hat so important? Try these experiments:

Staying warm: Pour two cups of hot tea or water. Cover one with a saucer and leave the second one uncovered. Wait five minutes, then check the cups. Which is hotter?

Keeping cool: Pour two cups of cold water and put them in the sun. Cover one cup with the saucer, and leave the second one uncovered. Wait ten minutes, then check the cups. Which is cooler?

Right — the cup with the "hat" kept warmer in the cold and cooler in the sun. The same is true for you. That's why, when you're feeling either too warm or too cold, you should put on a hat!

Rainwear

A poncho is a great item to pack if you're expecting rain —
it will cover both you and your pack. If you don't have a
poncho, a raincoat with hood and duck bill (attached to the
hood) will keep you dry and prevent the rain from dripping
down your face.

Or you could take a large plastic garbage bag, make three
holes — one head, two arms — and wear it as a raincoat. It
won't last long, but it can help in a pinch.

Your feet pose the biggest problem when caught in the rain.
Rain boots are a serious pain to hike in, but don't let that
stop you. Hiking in the rain can be as much fun as hiking
under a blazing sun. If you're caught in the rain, try this:
wrap your feet in plastic bags and jam them back into your
shoes.

TRAIL GRUB

Ten minutes into the hike and guess what — you have the munchies! Unless you're hiking in the city, the only munchables you'll find are in your pack. Try to pack "energy food" — nutritious, delicious and compact. Remember, you have to tote this stuff around!

Trail Mix

An energy-packed treat. You can vary the recipe if you have allergies — leave out the nuts, for instance. Use a handful each of:

— shelled sunflower seeds
— nuts (peanuts, cashews, walnuts)
— raisins
— dried cereal
— dried fruit (dates, bananas, apricots, etc.)
— M & Ms (optional)

Toss together and seal in a reusable container.

Other great hiking snacks to bring along:

- PBJs (the classic peanut butter and jam sandwich)
- frozen juice boxes (these can act as ice packs and you'll have a nice cold drink at lunch time)
- M&Ms (great for hot weather since they don't melt)
- GORP (a mix of Good Old Raisins and Peanuts)
- fruit or snack bars
- cheese and cracker snack packs
- nuts (unsalted)
- hard boiled eggs
- pepperoni or beef jerky sticks
- tuna or sardines (in easy-open cans)
- a bag of your favorite dry cereal (Option: put the cereal in a plastic container with a tight lid. Add a few tablespoons of powdered milk. On the trail simply add water, mix and presto — cereal and milk. Don't forget to bring a spoon!)

FIRST AID

First-Aid Kit

Buy it. St. John's Ambulance
has great portable first-aid kits.
So do hiking stores and drug
stores. Or make your own.
Your parents can help.

Include:

- ☐ **adhesive bandages, such as Band-Aids, in
  different sizes**

- ☐ **triangular bandages**

- ☐ **moleskins (like bandages but fuzzy on top —
  great for padding shoes to prevent sore feet)**

- ☐ **antiseptic and soap**

- ☐ **tweezers**

- ☐ **safety pins**

- ☐ **gauze**

- ☐ **elastic bandage for sprains**

- ☐ **adhesive tape**

- ☐ **scissors**

- ☐ **a first-aid book**

Talk it over with your parents — they might suggest
a mild pain remedy be included. Likewise, any
special medical supplies (for allergies to plants or
insect stings, or medical conditions such as asthma)
will have to be packed in the kit.

Injuries

There should be a first-aid book in your kit that explains how to properly treat basic injuries such as cuts, sprains, and even broken bones. It's also a great idea to take a first aid course if possible. The following provides a description of basic injury treatment:

- Stay calm. If you panic, so will the injured person.
- Do not move the person.
- Check first for bleeding, then for breathing, then for any broken bones.
- Stop any bleeding by applying pressure.
- Watch for shock (patient feels weak, has difficulty forming sentences, skin is cold and clammy, pulse is weak and rapid).
- Keep the patient warm. (If you are sure nothing is broken put something under as well as over the patient.)
- Loosen any tight clothing — belt, shoes, collar, etc.
- Decide who should go for help.

Don't leave an injured person alone if you can help it. If there are four of you, two can go for help. If you are in a group of three or two, it's almost always best to stay together, unless help is very close. Use your whistle and signals to call for help, and remember, since you told your parents where you are and when you'll be back, help will be coming soon!

Be sure to read your first-aid book before the hike.

FIRST AID

FINDING YOUR WAY

The Plan

How far should you hike? Take your time. Plan on covering about 1.5 km an hour. Add time for lunch, experiments, or just goofing off. Give yourself five minutes every half hour to stop and sniff the flowers. Remember, the purpose of a hike is not to get somewhere fast, but to enjoy the journey. Plan to get home an hour before sunset — at least!

Little Brothers and Sisters

Don't let little ones charge on ahead or take the lead. They might get lost and danger could be around the next bend. Small children should stay in the middle of a group and not be left to tag along at the end of the line.

Don't get carried away and hike too far. You may become too tired to walk back.

■

When you plan your hike, remember to allow enough time to get back home before sunset.

■

Don't hitchhike home. If you must, call home for a ride.

■

Stay off railway tracks and bridges and out of storm sewers.

■

Don't walk close to the edge of a river, stream, or lake.

18

Taking Breaks

It's a good idea to stop every 15 minutes. Make sure everyone, especially little kids, has a drink of water each time you stop. Remember that little kids can get tired very suddenly, then they have to be carried.

Directions

Remember: the sun rises in the East and sets in the West. At noon, it's hard to tell, but at other times of the day you can get an idea of your direction from the sun. Here's a trick to help you remember: the sun rises *Early* in the *East* and sets *Well* in the *West*.

The Compass

The earth behaves just like a big magnet. With a compass we use the North magnetic pole to guide us. To head North, we head in the direction that the marked end of the compass needle points toward.

How do we find East, South and West or any direction in between? Read on to find out.

Using Your Compass

A compass also contains what is known as the "compass rose." This is the spoked diagram on which the needle

Never go hiking off the trail in an unfamiliar area unless you have a map and compass and you are an expert at using them.

■

If your group plans to wander off the beaten trail, mark your path with chalk. Simply X the trees as you tromp though the forest. If you put your mark on the far side of trees as you pass them, they'll be easier to spot on the way back.

turns. It is like the face of a watch but instead of numbers to mark hours, it has letters that stand for directions. N = North, E = East, S = South, W = West.

Some compasses also have numbers dividing the circle of the compass into 360 equal sections called "degrees." These are for very fine and specific direction finding.

To use the compass to find a direction, for example East:

- Line up the compass so that the needle is pointing toward the N (for North).

- Draw an imaginary line from the centre point of the compass/needle to E (for East). That line will point East.

West will be in the exact opposite direction of East, and South the exact opposite direction of North.

Science in a backpack

Try this compass test.

You will need:

☐ **a compass**

☐ **a sweater, hat or other object to mark a spot**

☐ **a field or other open area**

Start in the center of the open space. Drop your hat or something else to mark your starting spot.

- Go North 5 paces. Stop.
- Go West 10 paces. Stop.
- Go South 20 paces. Stop.
- Go East 15 paces. Stop.

- Go North 15 paces Stop.
- Go West five paces. Stop.
- Look down. You should be back where you started.

Make Your Own Compass

You will need:

- [ ] a magnet
- [ ] a small needle
- [ ] a cork
- [ ] a bowl of water

- Rub the needle with the magnet for a couple of minutes and it will become lightly magnetized.

- Push the needle through the cork so its back and front end stick out of the cork about the same distance and needle and cork are well balanced.

- Sit the cork on the water in the bowl. It should turn so the needle points North to South. There's your compass.

Is it time to head home? There's an easy way to estimate the time left before sunset. Stand facing the setting sun. (Never stare directly into the sun.) Extend your arm. Bend your wrist in, thumb up. Put your hand between the sun and the horizon. Each finger is worth 15 minutes. If all four fingers just fit between the sun and the horizon then you have one hour of sunlight left. Head home!

Map Reading

There are road maps for cars, navigation maps for boats, and weather maps that help us decide how we should dress for the day. And, of course, there are maps for hikers.

The map should tell you two things:

- the direction of North (knowing North you can figure out the rest)
- the scale of the map

Most maps of the outdoors provide a picture scale in addition to a numeric scale. For example:

1 km   10 km

This kind of scale makes measuring distances easy. Just place a piece of string, pipe cleaner or a twig down on the map, along your route. Then measure it against the scale to calculate how far you have to go.

Using Your Map to Find a Direction

- Lay the map out on flat ground and find the arrow that points North. (Most outdoor maps will have a large arrow, or even a full compass rose, somewhere on them.)
- Line up your compass so that the needle points toward the North on the compass. Lay the compass on the map.
- Holding the compass still, turn the map so that the North arrow on the map points in the same direction as the needle on the compass.

You can now use your map to tell you what lies in each direction around you.

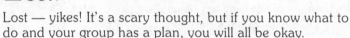

When you take a break mid-hike, agree on some rules. Little kids should stay in sight at all times. No one should wander out of whistle range. Set a time to regroup and hike on.

Lost!

Lost — yikes! It's a scary thought, but if you know what to do and your group has a plan, you will all be okay.

Discuss your lost and found plan before the hike. We suggest a plan called Hug-A-Tree. The plan is simple — if you can't find your hiking mates, find the nearest big tree and give it a hug. Try to pick a tree on dry higher ground. Next, blast your whistle three times. Now, stay put! Don't be embarrassed, and don't think that everyone is just over the next hill. This can get you really lost.

If You're Lost

Remember — if you stay where you are you'll be found in no time. If time passes, don't panic. Here are some suggestions:

- Collect some branches to sit on. The ground may become cold and damp.
- Build a shelter or a lean-to (it will give you something to do, if nothing else).

- Is there a snack in your pack? Don't eat it — not yet anyway. The trick is to make sure other animals don't eat it either. Suspend your pack from a nearby tree. (Don't toss it up — you may never get it back down!) Hang it from a low-slung branch.
- Talk to the tree (no one can hear you), sing, whistle, hum.
- Note everything about your tree in your nature notebook.
- Wait. (The hard part.)
- Practice your knot tying techniques (see page 119).
- Read everything in this book and your first-aid book too.

Little brothers and sisters are most likely to wander off and get lost during a rest period, lunch break, or while you are doing experiments. You might mark out a play area with string. But nothing replaces keeping a sharp eye on them.

■

When you're hiking, put a couple of meters between you and your hiking buddies to prevent branches from swinging back and whacking the hiker behind you.

To make a lean-to:

- Tie a piece of rope to a low tree branch.
- Tie the other end to a sturdy stick and push it into the ground or weigh the rope down with a rock or a log.
- Drape your space blanket or poncho over the rope.
- Weigh down the corners with rocks. Presto — instant shelter!

If Someone Else Is Lost

If you turn around and find that a member of your group is missing, *everyone* must backtrack in an organized manner to find him or her.

Remember, listen for calls or sounds of a whistle!

We don't recommend that kids start fires to attract attention. Small fires can lead to big fires!

■

Three puffs on a whistle should always mean emergency.

Sound Signals

It's a good idea to agree on some emergency whistle codes before you begin your hike. Don't make it too complicated, though, or you're liable to forget.

- two blows — all right or "I hear you"
- three blows — emergency

If you don't have a whistle, call out every few minutes. Too much yelling might mean that you lose your voice when you need it most. Another alternative: find two pieces of wood and bang them together every few minutes. Three clapping sounds at a time means emergency.

Ground Signals

If you are on high, bald ground, collect sticks and make one of these emergency signals. Each one should be at least 15 cm high.

- X — unable to proceed, or you are staying put
- 1 — HELP, doctor required

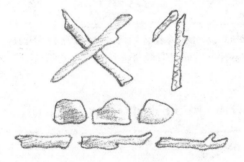

Three of anything — three sticks in a row, three rocks in a row — also means "help." If you are lost and you hear a plane overhead, you could try "mirror flashing." Hold your mirror up near one eye, with the mirror-side facing out. Extend your other hand and make a V with two fingers. Use these two fingers as a "sight." Catch the sun by tilting the mirror and reflecting it back through your two fingers. Drop your fingers as soon as you focus the reflection.

WEATHER

What's the weather going to be like for your hike? Will it rain?

Plants, animals and insects are very sensitive to weather conditions. Legends and folklore are plentiful too. Do you know which of the following are true and which are not?

If rain is on the way, many flowers fold up their leaves or petals.

True. Clover, for example, folds its leaves and dandelions and tulips fold their petals.

Spiders sometimes haul in their webs before the rain starts.

True.

Some trees turn over their leaves before the rain to keep the tops dry.

True. Red and silver maples, and poplars, do this.

Ants travel in lines before a rainstorm and scatter in dry weather.

False.

Cows gather and bed down in the pasture before a storm.

True.

Bees fly in circles before a rainstorm.

False, but they do stay closer to the hive.

If a house fly pesters you, rain is coming.

True.

Dogs sniff the air more often before a rainstorm.

True.

Noises are clearer and smells are stronger before it rains.

True.

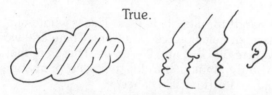

A rooster crowing at night means rain in the morning.

False.

Of course, you can easily turn on the radio to check the weather. If crackly static is all you get — turn the radio off and get ready for a thunderstorm. Electrical static from nearby lightning may be interfering with the radio waves.

Pssst, want to know a secret? You can tell how far away the lightning is by counting the seconds between the lightning and thunder and dividing by three. That's approximately how far away in kilometers the lightning is. What if you see lightning and hear thunder at the same time? Look out — the storm is overhead.

Sun Info

You've probably already heard about UV rays and SPF. But what do these initials mean and why are they important?

SPF stands for "sun protection factor" found in sunscreen products. The higher the SPF number on the package the greater the protection. Always use sunscreen when spending time outdoors. On a hike you'll want to use a sunscreen with a minimum SPF of 15.

UV stands for ultraviolet rays. This is what your sunscreen helps protect you from. There are two to be aware of: UVB and UVA rays. These are the ones that cause tanning, burning, wrinkles, premature aging and certain skin cancers.

Sunscreen Tips:

- Choose waterproof and odorless sunscreen. Scented sunscreen may attract bugs.
- Apply the sunscreen half an hour before you leave home.
- Don't forget to apply sunscreen to the tips of your ears, nose, lips and the back of your neck, as well as any other exposed areas.
- Be sure to put enough sunscreen on exposed areas. Half a handful is about right if you're wearing long pants.

Sun Smarts

Answer true or false to the following:

1 A tan can be healthy.
☐ TRUE ☐ FALSE

2 A tan can protect you from getting a sunburn.
☐ TRUE ☐ FALSE

3 Black skin cannot burn.
☐ TRUE ☐ FALSE

4 You can't get burned when swimming.
☐ TRUE ☐ FALSE

5 A T-shirt will always protect you from a burn.
☐ TRUE ☐ FALSE

6 Most skin cancers happen to adults so kids don't have to worry.
☐ TRUE ☐ FALSE

7 You can only get burned in sunny weather.
☐ TRUE ☐ FALSE

Answers:

1) False.

2) False.

3) False. Black skin only has an SPF of 8 or so.

4) False. The water's reflection may even intensify the burn.

5) False. If you can see through a T-shirt, so can the sun.

6) False. Almost 80% of our exposure to sun happens in childhood. One of the conditions that put people at risk of cancer is a bad sunburn during childhood.

7) False. UV rays go right through clouds so you can get burned even on cloudy days.

Use a Cricket Thermometer

Crickets are very sensitive to the weather. They also have rhythm. You can estimate the temperature by listening to the number of times a cricket chirps in one minute.

You will need:

☐ a watch

☐ pencil and paper

- Count the number of chirps you hear in a 15-second period.
- Divide this number by 2, then add 6.

The answer you get is the temperature in degrees Celsius.

The number you end up with isn't exact and can vary between species of cricket but it's a fun experiment. Test how accurate the crickets in your area are.

Thunder and Lightning

Hiking in the rain can be fun. Dodging lightning bolts is *not* fun.

If you're caught on the trail during a thunderstorm, stay out from under tall trees, get out of the water and crouch down low until the storm passes. Only your feet should touch the ground. Don't hold onto anyone and take your pack off in case there is metal inside. Avoid high ground and flat open spaces if possible.

Here's how lightning works. Tiny droplets of water in a cloud pick up an electrical charge. The greater the amount of water and air motion in a cloud, the greater the electrical charge that builds up.

A thundercloud builds up such a large amount of electrical charge that it gives off an enormous spark. FLASH! We've got lightning. The spark can jump from cloud to cloud or from cloud to earth.

The air along the streak of lightning is heated. It expands outward with the force of an explosion. BOOM! We've got thunder.

Did you know that lightning is similar to the electrical charge you get when touching something metal after walking across a carpet? Lightning is much, much, much more powerful though.

By the way, lightning can strike twice in the same place — the CN Tower in Toronto is hit by lightning about 65 times a year!

Clouds

Forget the hike for a minute. Lie on the ground and look up. You might be able to see faces or shapes. Where? In the clouds, of course.

Clouds can be classified into three main types:

Cirrus clouds — wispy clouds, high up. They are made up of tiny ice crystals. They pose little threat of rain.

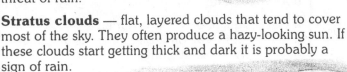

Stratus clouds — flat, layered clouds that tend to cover most of the sky. They often produce a hazy-looking sun. If these clouds start getting thick and dark it is probably a sign of rain.

Cumulus clouds — billowy and bushy, they look like big balls of cotton. They are generally signs of good weather. Thunderclouds are cumulus clouds that have grown big, dark and mean. Rain and lightning are on the way!

Finally the rain has stopped. A miracle happens — a rainbow. Do you know what causes a rainbow? Sunlight is white — or what we think of as white — but within the "white" are lots of colors. When a beam of light passes through the water in the air, the beam is bent and the colors inside are exposed.

BUG ATTACK!

Mosquitoes

Mosquitoes bite all day but tend to munch most at dawn, dusk and on overcast days. Apply insect repellent every few hours and wear long sleeves and long pants.

Black-flies

Black-flies attack all day long but especially at dusk and dawn. Areas around the collar and hairline are particularly tasty to this tiny, nasty bug. The bite itself isn't painful but the red, swollen spot left behind can be. Hint: rub on calamine lotion and see a doctor if the bite becomes inflamed and very painful.

Sand Flies

(Also called midges or no-see-ems.) These pesky bugs are so little they can hardly be seen. Still they give a nasty, itchy bite.

Did you know

that how you smell may attract bugs? After you eat a banana your skin gives off an odor that mosquitoes find yummy. Garlic, on the other hand, has been known to ward off bugs — and other hikers. A bath or shower is important before a hike because bugs like smelly people. But don't wash your hair in scented shampoo or use flowery smelling soap — bugs are attracted to perfumes.

Ticks

Ticks burrow under skin to get at your blood. If a tick does embed itself in your skin, tell an adult. The tick should be pulled out gently, not squeezed, and the area treated with antiseptic.

Bees

The yellow and black coloring of the bee is meant to warn its enemies to stay clear, so take note and do likewise. A bee hardly ever stings unless it, or its nest, is under attack or it mistakes your flowered shirt (and therefore you) for a flower. Tell an adult if you have been stung and remove the stinger by scraping across the area with a thin, flat object (like a credit card).

Wasps and Hornets

Wasps and hornets can sting several times. Treat the sting with a cold compress, antiseptic and calamine lotion.

Allergies to Insect Stings

Violent reactions to stings are rare but serious. If one of your hiking buddies gets stung and shows any of these symptoms, forget the hike. Get to a doctor fast:

- hives, rash or itchiness all over the body
- difficulty breathing
- nausea, vomiting

BUGS

- diarrhea
- swelling of eyelids, lips, tongue, difficulty swallowing
- fast heartbeat
- fainting
- seizures

If you are allergic, you know that you must carry your medication at all times. Tell your friends about your allergy before you head out. Show them your medication and give them instructions on how to use it. Always wear a MedicAlert bracelet.

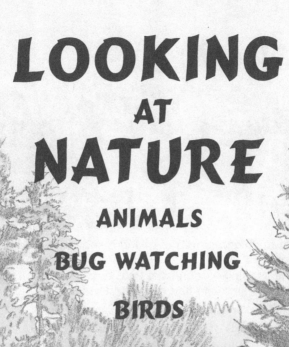

LOOKING
AT
NATURE

ANIMALS

BUG WATCHING

BIRDS

ROCKS

WILDFLOWERS

ANIMALS

One of the biggest thrills of hiking is spotting a wild animal. Although the woods are full of creatures, they are very good at keeping hidden from you. Even if you don't see any wildlife, you can find tracks and other signs that they have been there.

If you find signs of an animal, be quiet and still. Look carefully around. If you spy something, slowly bring your binoculars up for a closer look.

If you do see an animal, remember — don't approach it or try to lure it out into the open with food! Even the cutest and most harmless-looking furry creatures will attack or bite if they are cornered. Raccoons, weasels, otters, badgers, beavers and possums have sharp teeth and claws. Porcupines will whack you with their spiny tails and leave quills sticking in you. Foxes and wolves, both relatives of the dog, can inflict painful bites. And any of these creatures can carry diseases such as rabies.

It's unlikely that you'll come across a poisonous snake on your hike but if you do, remember that snakes strike when they are cornered. Watch where you're walking and be careful about picking up things or reaching into places that might be good hiding spots for snakes or other creatures.

If you are confronted by an angry animal, back up slowly. Even if an animal isn't a threat to you, *you* can be a threat to *it!* Remember, you're in the animal's home. Replace any logs and rocks you

> ## Did you know
> a skunk can spray you from up to three meters away?

overturn, and be especially careful of nests and baby animals. If you get between a mother and her brood, watch out! She'll get really nasty to protect her young.

Feeding Signs

- holes in trees
- sap
- holes in mud
- nipped and chewed twigs
- scratched or bare logs and tree trunks
- feathers
- pine cone scales
- opened nuts

Signs of Animal Homes

- holes in trees
- burrows in ground
- matted plants
- nests
- holes in river banks

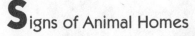

Animal Tracks and Trails

- droppings
- shed fur, snake skins or feathers
- sounds

Stalking

The woods are full of trails, from tiny ones made by chipmunks to large ones used by deer. If you keep the wind in your face, the animals you're stalking won't smell you. Stay well back and use your binoculars so you aren't seen.

Identifying Animal Tracks

Identifying animals by their tracks can be challenging and fun. The following are some of the tracks you may see on your hike:

rabbit

skunk

brown bear

raccoon

porcupine

wolf

fox

black bear

badger

moose

deer

NOT TO SCALE

Make a Cast of an Animal Track

You will need:

☐ a large plastic pop bottle

☐ a can, pail or bowl for mixing

☐ plaster of paris

☐ a few cups of water

☐ a small trowel, spade or shovel

- Before setting out on your hike cut the plastic pop bottle into rings about 2.5 cm wide. Bring three or four of the rings, as well as the other items, with you on the hike.

- Tracks are best found where the ground is soft and muddy. Look for tracks that are well formed. Select one and place a plastic ring around it.

- Mix the plaster of paris in the can until it's thick but still runny. Pour the mixture gently into the track and fill the ring.

- Let it sit for 15 minutes or so until the plaster has hardened. Carefully dig up the cast and wrap it in old cloth or newspaper. When you get home, allow the cast to harden completely, at least a few more hours. Then remove the ring and gently wash the cast.

- If you press the cast into plasticine you will see the track as you originally did outdoors.

- Don't forget to find out what kind of animal the track belongs to. Label your cast.

* BUG WATCHING

Insects, spiders, centipedes, worms and so on may be small, but they are fascinating creatures. There are over 100,000 kinds in North America alone, and they live everywhere: in forests, fields, swamps, cities, even underwater. Wherever you go, you're sure to see lots of them on your hike. Have your magnifying glass ready — you'll need it.

Ants

No need to go looking for ants. Have lunch in a grassy area and they'll find you! Ants are social, which means that they work together. Put an apple or other juicy treat on the ground and watch them come running.

Ladybugs

Do you think ladybugs bring good luck? Who knows? But if you see one make a wish, just in case. Ladybugs are beetles. Farmers and gardeners love them because they eat other insect pests.

Spiders

There are thousands of different kinds of spiders and most are harmless. Just to be on the safe side, if you have a rest and decide to take off your shoes, give each shoe a good shake before slipping it back on. Spiders like to hide in smelly, dark places such as shoes.

Butterflies

How can you tell the difference between a butterfly and a moth? Butterflies fly about by day; moths fly at night. Butterflies have skinny antennae; moths have fuzzy feelers. At rest, butterfly wings point up; moth wings lie flat on their backs.

Did you know

that ants can lift 50 times their weight? That's a little like you being able to lift a compact car!

■

that the Monarch butterfly migrates south every fall, a journey of more than 3,000 kms?

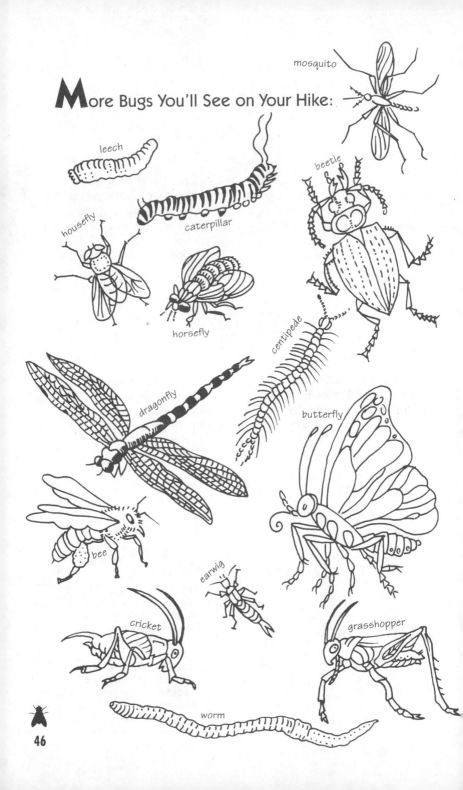

More Bugs You'll See on Your Hike:

mosquito

leech

caterpillar

beetle

housefly

horsefly

centipede

dragonfly

butterfly

bee

earwig

cricket

grasshopper

worm

Watching Bugs

You will need:

- [ ] a magnifying glass

- [ ] a clear plastic container

- [ ] tweezers for picking up bugs

The plastic container is for catching and holding bug specimens. Many nature stores carry "bug boxes" which combine the box and a magnifier in one.

Next, you need to find some bugs. You might say that bugs don't need to be found — just look at all those pesky ants and mosquitoes! These bugs are easy to spot, but many others are shy or well camouflaged.

Try examining a rotted log. If you dig into it carefully, you can find a whole world inside. Or choose a tree and look at it with your magnifying glass, from the earth around the roots to the ends of the branches. You'll find bugs, larvae (their young), trails left by munchers, even eggs!

Turn over a rock and look — quickly — to see all the life underneath.

Remember: always leave the area exactly as you found it. That includes replacing any logs or stones you have moved.
If you are taking insects home for further study, make careful note of what they are feeding on. Be sure you have enough of the right food for the insect.

Always return the insect to the place you found it.

BIRDS

Birdwatching is a great hiking activity — why not plan a birding break part way through your hike? This is when your binoculars will come in handy. Stop, be still, listen and watch.

You can spot birds almost anywhere — in parks, ponds, rivers, beaches, fields and in the forest. Look for them:

- on the ground
- along tree branches, tree trunks, treetops
- around fallen logs
- on or around rocks
- around flowers or grass in fields
- on shorelines
- around marsh vegetation

You will need:

☐ **binoculars**

☐ **your nature notebook**

☐ **a pencil**

☐ **a camera (optional)**

☐ **a field guide to birds**

Although you can spot birds all year long, the best time of year for birdwatching is spring or fall, during migration periods. The best time of day is early morning or early evening. If you hear a bird close by but can't see it, try *spishing* — just say "spish"! (Think of spishing as saying "Pssssst" to get someone's attention. We can't tell you how or why it works, only that it does!)

Get up before the birds. As you listen in the pre-dawn light, you'll hear different birds waking and calling out. One lone bird will start, followed by another, then another. It will be daylight before you hear all the birds singing together — and not always in harmony either. Some birds can sing between 15 and 25 different "songs" — and not forget a beat.

Another fun thing to do is identify the birds you see and then keep count of how many you've spotted (some avid birdwatchers have listed up to 500 different sightings!). This is where your notebook and field guide come in handy. Record the place you spotted the bird. Then ask yourself these questions:

- What shape and size is the bird?
- What color is it?
- What kind of markings does it have?
- Does it have a song?
- What shape is its beak? (This can give you a clue to its eating habits!)

Did you know that about 645 species of bird live in North America? There are about 8,600 species in the whole world.

- How does it fly — does it soar in a straight line, glide, hover or flit back and forth?

Your field guide will help you identify and learn about what you see.

STRAIGHT LINE

GLIDING

BOUNCING

HOVERING

Describe a Bird's Habitat

The kinds of birds you can find depends on the area you are in. Look around you, and describe the habitat — the area in which the bird lives. What sort of food supply is available? From this you can predict what kinds of birds you might see. For example, you'll want to look for:

- hummingbirds where there are wildflowers
- woodpeckers in a forest
- red-wing blackbirds and goldfinches in meadows
- herons and ducks in a marsh
- hawks circling high above meadows and fields
- owls (probably sleeping ones) in heavy woods

Now close your eyes and listen hard for birdsong. Once you hear a bird, turn your head slowly toward it. Then open your eyes and spot your bird!

Bird Behavior

In the spring the male bird chooses a nesting site. He claims his territory by singing. His song not only warns off other male birds but also

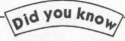

attracts a mate. Once the male has spotted a potential mate he puts on a show: the American goldfinch sings while zipping around in circles; the red-winged blackbird shows off its colors. If you know what to look for you'll see all the action for yourself.

Birds' Nests

Birds build nests in the spring to lay their eggs and raise their young. Some of the materials they use are sticks, grass, moss, bark, straw, animal hair and even spider webs.

Some birds, such as Whip-poor-wills, make no nest at all! Instead, they lay their eggs right on the ground. Watch where you're walking!

Some birds build hanging nests, others nest in the hollows of trees, some nestle their nests in strong branches, others nest in rock crevices or hollow ground. Nests can also be found in the sides of cliffs, under the eaves of buildings or even on top of hydro poles! Looking for nests in the forest is easiest in the fall when the leaves have fallen. Do not disturb the nests. Peek if you can, but never touch!

Identifying Nests

Once you do locate a nest, use your field guide to help you find out what kind of bird may have built it. Be careful, though, a deserted nest may have become home to another animal or bird.

More Birds You May See on Your Hike

Loons are well-known for their beautiful but eerie call. They can be found close to their breeding grounds, usually in inland waters. In flight, look for a sloped-down neck.

The great blue **heron** is best known for its towering stature. Herons can often be spotted spearing fish with their long bills in lakes, streams, marshes and swamps.

Despite the many varieties, **geese** can usually be identified by their loud honking call. Flocks fly in a V-formation. The Canada goose is the most common variety in North America.

Some **ducks** feed by bobbing their heads into water, others dive underwater for their food. Some have green heads, some have purple heads. Make note of their differences and see how many kinds of ducks you can spot!

Gulls and **terns** are often found on coasts, oceans, lakes and rivers. Again, there are many different varieties of both. There's even a "laughing" gull! You can easily recognize terns because of their bright orange beaks.

A **hawk** — you'll know it by its seemingly effortless soaring and diving in search of prey. Hawks nest in conifers, hollow trees, rock crevices or on marshy ground.

Grouse and **pheasants** are mostly found in woodland areas. One type of grouse makes a beating sound on its chest to show off! You can often spot them on the ground in forests.

You'll be lucky if you spot an **owl** on your hike — some kinds of owls only come out at night. If you do see one, it could be an angry screech owl that wants you to get away from its nest!

Hummingbirds are found in many different habitats, usually hovering over flowers to feed on nectar.

Woodpeckers prefer wooded areas. You're likely to hear one hammering at a tree before you see it, however. (Did you know that the yellow-bellied sapsucker is a type of woodpecker?)

Swallows can often be spotted swooping or diving near lakes, marshes, streams and even inside open buildings such as barns. They feed on insects and berries.

Jays — look for their distinctive blue coloring and their fanned tails and heads.

A **thrush** can usually be heard before it is seen. You can often spot them in woodland areas, feeding on the ground.

Warblers are very small birds that you're more likely to hear than to see. The many varieties are found in marsh and woodland areas.

Don't recognize a certain bird? Quick, draw it in your field notebook. Make a note of the colors, time of day you spotted it and its behavior. Then see if you can find it in your field guide.

Feather Collection

Bird feathers can be found everywhere, but especially on the ground under a nest. Gather up the feathers and make a scrapbook. As you are taping the feathers into your book, notice how the hollow shaft in the centre of the feather has rows of tiny teeth. These bind together like a zipper. Birds "do up their zippers" when they preen themselves. Classify the feathers in your scrapbook. You could organize them by color, size or where you found them. Can you tell what type of bird they are from?

Different Types of Feathers:

- Contour feathers are long and stiff. They cover the outside of the body and tail.
- Filoplumes are tiny, soft feathers at the base of the contour feather.
- Down feathers are under the large contour feathers. Very soft, they keep the bird warm.
- Powder-down feathers have a thin film on them. This helps the birds keep themselves clean.

Don't forget to wash your hands after handling feathers!

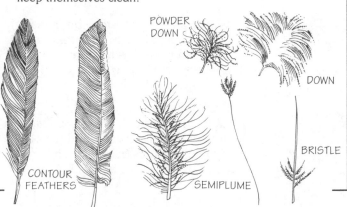

POWDER DOWN

DOWN

CONTOUR FEATHERS

SEMIPLUME

BRISTLE

Rocks

If you plan to collect rocks on your hike, take small samples and label them as you go. Some samples, such as fossils, may be delicate. Wrap them in a piece of paper or your bandana before plunking them into your pack. Make notes in your nature notebook about where you picked up each sample. See if you can identify them when you get home.

You will need:

- [ ] goggles (old swimming or woodshop goggles should do)
- [ ] a sturdy bag
- [ ] a marker
- [ ] masking tape
- [ ] your nature notebook
- [ ] a pencil
- [ ] a hammer
- [ ] an old sock (no holes, please)

Did you know

that if your hiking area is mainly sedimentary rock, it was probably under water at one time!

■

that crystals are minerals that come in regular geometric shapes? A good example is salt — look at it under a magnifying glass or microscope. What shape is it?

■

that some dinosaurs swallowed stones to help digest their food? Some birds do too!

There are three main types of rock: igneous, sedimentary and metamorphic.

Igneous Rock

Igneous rocks are the oldest rocks on earth, and more are being formed all the time — volcano lava is one example. Igneous rocks were made from molten magma in the center of the earth, which cooled as it got to the earth's surface. If you see traces of igneous rock around, look up. Was that hill once a volcano?

How to recognize them:

All igneous rocks have crystals in them. Some crystals are so tiny you can only see them with a magnifying glass, but others can be easily seen with the naked eye.

Sedimentary Rock

Rocks are very hard, but weather still wears them down over time. Tiny particles of rocks and living matter settle in low-lying areas, often under the sea. Layers and layers build up, and eventually they become a mass of solid rock again.

Metamorphic Rock

Metamorphic rocks were all either igneous or sedimentary rocks at one time. Then extreme heat or pressure, or both, made them change form. To understand

How to recognize them:

Sedimentary rocks are made of layers of particles, large or small. The layers are often easy to see. Sedimentary rocks are the only rocks that contain fossils. If you put a drop of water on a sedimentary rock, it will eventually soak in.

how metamorphic rocks form, picture a bag of marshmallows and imagine that they are rocks. If you put pressure on them, they will squish together to form a big mass with fewer air bubbles. Or, if you put heat on them by toasting, they melt and change color.

Rock Collecting and Classifying

If you find interesting rocks, take *small* samples. Rocks make your backpack very heavy, very fast!

Because wind and weather can change the outside appearance of a rock, it is sometimes necessary to crack the rock with a hammer to get a more accurate picture of it. Put the rock in the old sock you brought with you, then hit it with the hammer. The sock will prevent chips from flying everywhere. You should wear your goggles though, just in case. Oh, and be very careful not to hit your fingers.

Put a small piece of masking tape on each sample. Use your marker to label where you got it. When you get home, you can then classify your rocks further.

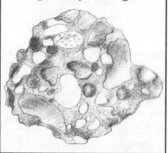

You can classify rocks by:

- scratch colour (rub the rock on a piece of unglazed tile, and note the colour of the streak it makes. Or scratch the rock itself with a hard object and note the colour of the scratch.)
- transparency
- smell
- feel
- magnetism
- hardness

Where to Look for Rocks

On a forest hike, look for rocks next to streams, where a variety of rocks collect; where roads cut through the countryside, exposing rock faces; on cliff faces.

You can find lots of different kinds of rocks in the city, too — marble, granite and slate are just some of the the rocks used in building.

Don't climb up cliffs to examine rocks — use your binoculars!

What kind of rock is common to your area or the area of your hike? Knowing whether it's mostly igneous, sedimentary or metamorphic will give you an idea of the long-term natural history of the area.

Fossils

If you find yourself in an area of sedimentary rocks, see if you can spot a fossil! You probably won't find a dinosaur, but tiny prehistoric seashells and other creatures might be visible. If the rock isn't small enough to pick up, just make a fossil print in your nature notebook and note the place and date you found it.

Did you know

that you can learn about science just by sucking a candy? As you suck, even a bumpy, hard candy will become smooth and oblong or round. This is exactly what happens to jagged or pointy rocks after many hundreds, possibly thousands of years of waves and wind brushing over them.

Fossil Prints

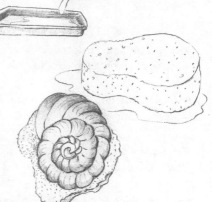

You will need:

☐ **fossil**

☐ **paint**

☐ **sponge and pan**

☐ **thick paper**

- Put the sponge in a tray and soak it with paint.
- Dip the fossil into the painted sponge and "print" it on the paper.

Or, you can press the fossil into self-hardening clay for a special effect.

Science in a backpack

Sometimes sand contains traces of iron.
Here's a simple way to find out if it does.

You will need:

☐ **a magnet**

☐ **one or more samples of sand**

- Pass the magnet over the sand and watch if bits of iron leap up and cling to the magnet.

If you haven't brought a magnet with you, use your jar to collect some sand and try the experiment at home.

Rock Display

- Show off your rock collection on a shelf at home. (Dab a little mineral oil on each rock to give it that shiny "wet" look.)

- Personalize large rocks with paint or write a quote on them and use as paperweights or door stops.

- Keep the rocks in a clear glass jar filled with water. The colors will show up well.

- Put pebbles and small stones on the bottom of your aquarium. (Wash them well first!)

- Make a pebble picture. Sort out the different colors. Make a drawing on a piece of cardboard. Decorate the drawing with your pebbles. Varnish the entire picture.

- Take a shoe box lid and glue small rock samples to it. Label and display it at home or school.

WILDFLOWERS

If you plan to look for wildflowers on your hike, you will need:

- ☐ a magnifying glass
- ☐ your nature notebook
- ☐ a pencil
- ☐ a measuring tape
- ☐ a camera (optional)
- ☐ a wildflower handbook

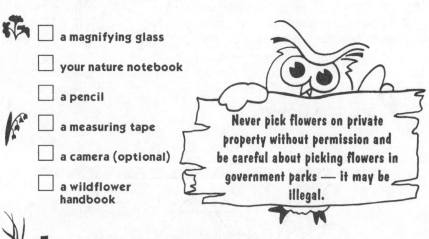

Never pick flowers on private property without permission and be careful about picking flowers in government parks — it may be illegal.

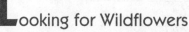

Looking for Wildflowers

Record the time and date of your find in your nature notebook. Include a quick sketch as well. If you want to keep some samples, pick the flowers on a sunny day after the dew has dried. (Damp flowers do not press well.) You can buy a plant and flower press, or make your own!

- Keep a record of all the wildflowers you find. Sorting them by color is easiest.

- Draw the flower in your nature notebook, or take a quick photo. Note when and where you found it. Then add a brief description of the plant: the colour of the flower and leaves, the number and arrangement of leaves and petals, what the stem looks like, and anything else interesting about it. You could also measure its height.

- If your flower handbook is pocket-sized, you could bring it with you to identify flowers on the spot. Or you could wait and check once you get home.

If you are going to pick flowers for a press, be sure that it's legal to pick flowers in the area you're hiking. Then take just one, and don't trample the other flowers when you pick yours. Remember, if you take or damage them, they won't be there for others to enjoy!

Parts of a Flower

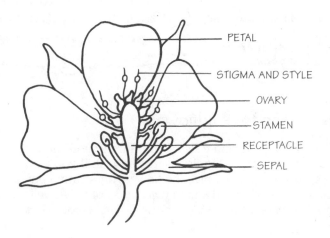

PETAL

STIGMA AND STYLE

OVARY

STAMEN

RECEPTACLE

SEPAL

Make Your Own Leaf and Flower Press

You will need:

- [ ] two pieces of wood, each about 15 cm square

- [ ] blotting paper or white construction paper
  (colored paper may leave color on your samples)

- [ ] squares of cardboard

- [ ] four long screws/washers/nuts

- [ ] an adult to help you

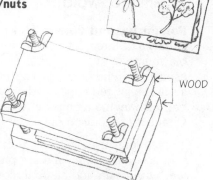

PAPER

WOOD

- Ask an adult to help you drill holes in the corners of the wood for the screws.
- Cut the pieces of paper and cardboard the same size as the wood. Cut off the corners so that the screws do not go through them.
- Lay a piece of paper on the bottom piece of wood. Arrange a flower on this, then cover with another piece of paper and a piece of cardboard. Repeat until the pile will just fit between the screws.
- Place the second piece of wood on top and use the washers and nuts to screw down firmly. Leave the flowers for at least a month.

Of course, you could create a quick press out of books (encyclopedias are great for this!). Put flowers or leaves

Don't eat berries, mushrooms or anything that you didn't bring with you. Even familiar berries found along the roadside may have been sprayed with harmful pesticides.

between two sheets of blotting paper or construction paper, and put them on top of a book. Then place several heavy books on top.

Or you can layer flowers between the pages of a discarded phone book, and put something heavy on top.

You can do lots of things with your pressed flowers — use them to decorate stationery, note cards, scrapbooks, bookmarks, whatever!

Plants to Avoid

POISON IVY

POISON OAK

POISON SUMAC

NETTLE

Poison Ivy and Poison Oak: "Leaves of three, let it be." That's an old rhyme worth remembering, especially if the leaves have smooth surfaces, jagged edges and grayish berries hanging alongside. What is it? Chances are, poison oak or poison ivy.

These plants usually grow as bushes. If you do touch either of these plants, wash your skin and all your clothes in hot, soapy water. See your doctor if any form of rash appears and if it does, try hard not to scratch. That only helps it spread.

Poison Sumac: This plant usually grows as a large shrub. You can recognize it by its greenish flowers and greenish-white berries (non-poisonous sumacs have red berries). Like its cousins poison ivy and poison oak, it produces an irritating oil that can cause an itchy rash on your skin.

Nettles: Full-grown nettles have hairy spikes that stick to whatever touches them. They will leave a burning sensation on skin that will last anywhere from a few minutes to few hours. Ouch!

Did you know

that because tall trees block out the sun, many woodland flowers bloom in early spring to catch what few rays they can?

■

that the dandelion is not native to North America? Early explorers brought it over from Europe.

FOREST

THE FOREST HIKE

You will need:

☐ binoculars

☐ a magnifying glass

☐ a plant press

One of the best places to hike is the forest. But first, stop and think. Think of your home, your bedroom, your club house — how would you feel if someone went through and wrecked your stuff? Right, you'd feel terrible.

Before you tromp through a forest leaving a path of destruction in your wake, remember just what it is you're tromping on. This is home to thousands of bugs, plants and animals! It's best to stay on marked trails. If none exists — step carefully.

Look before you touch or kick. What's under that rock or log? Maybe it's someone's home. You may hurt or kill an animal or insect. Or, you might get hurt yourself. How would you like to come face to face with a poisonous spider, a scorpion or an angry wasp?

Forest life

Life in the forest is all connected in some way or another. Each citizen of the forest has a role to play in its constant cycle of birth, life, death and rebirth. The various forms of life can be divided into four categories.

The Producers: trees and plants. Everything growing and green contains chlorophyll. This substance absorbs the sun's rays and through a process called photosynthesis creates oxygen. This oxygen, along with water, is released through the leaves.

Consumers: creatures like squirrels, rabbits and deer that eat plants.

Predators: meat-eaters such as foxes and hawks that eat small animals.

Decomposers: insects, worms and other tiny creatures that live on or under the soil. They clean up by breaking down dead plant and animal waste and mulching them into the soil. This enriches the soil, which in turn feeds the trees and other plant life.

Anatomy of a Forest

Forests can be divided into four layers: the tree layer, the shrub layer, the field layer and the ground layer.

↑tree
←shrub
←field
←ground

Tree Layer

There are two main types of trees: deciduous trees (also known as broadleaf trees) lose their leaves each fall, stay bare all winter, and grow new leaves in the spring. The leaves are generally broad and flat. Examples: maple, oak, elm and birch trees.

Coniferous trees grow their seeds in cones. They are also called evergreens, because they usually keep their leaves year-round. The leaves are generally needle-like. Examples: spruce, pine, hemlock, and cedar.

Did you know

that hundreds of millions of years ago, when dinosaurs ruled, some ferns grew as tall as trees and covered massive areas of land? In fact, the large coal fields that we now mine are the remnants of huge fern forests.

Shrub Layer

The shrub layer is made up mainly of bushes and small trees.

Shrubs can be described as a cross between trees and plants. They don't grow as tall as most trees but have similar woody stems. Generally, more than one equally strong stem rises from the same root system. Shrubs tend to grow less than five meters high. Bushes and small trees compete with larger trees for sunlight, water and food.

Field Layer

The field layer is the small plant life found in the forest. Included are wildflowers, ferns and very young trees called seedlings.

Ferns grow in moist areas. They look a little bit like small, flat pine trees, but they are actually more closely related to mosses.

Ferns reproduce by means of cells called spores. Look underneath fern leaves with your magnifying glass. Any little rusty patches you see are the spores.

Ground Layer

The ground layer is made up of all the plant life that grows very close to the ground, like mushrooms and other fungi, mosses, lichen and small plants. These don't need much light to grow.

Mushrooms are a type of fungus. Fungi do not contain chlorophyll, the green substance that helps most plants make food. Fungi have to absorb all of their food from their surroundings. You can find them growing on rotting logs.

Moss looks like a plush green carpet. Look closely with your magnifying glass to see the many tiny stems that make up the larger mat of moss.

Lichen (pronounced *like*-en) are often gray or green but sometimes yellow or red. They can often be found growing on tree trunks or rock faces.

Remember, always wash your hands thoroughly and carefully after touching wild mushrooms and never, ever taste them.

Make a Print from Mushroom Spores

Spores are how a mushroom reproduces. To see what spores look like, do the following.

You will need:

☐ **a gilled mushroom (the kind that you find in a store)**

☐ **a sheet of black construction paper**

☐ **a cup or jar to cover the mushroom to prevent drafts**

☐ **clear fixative (from an art supply shop) if you plan to keep your print**

- Carefully pick a mushroom and bring it home in a container.
- Set the construction paper flat. Remove the stem of the mushroom from the mushroom cap.
- Place the cap on the construction paper with the gilled or ribbed-looking side against the paper. Cover the mushroom with the cup so that the spores don't get blown away. Leave it for at least a few hours, or overnight.
- When you finally lift up the cup and the mushroom cap the spores will have left a pattern. Spray the paper with a clear fixative if you wish to preserve it.
- Try placing different kinds of mushroom caps on a single piece of paper. Do they make different patterns?

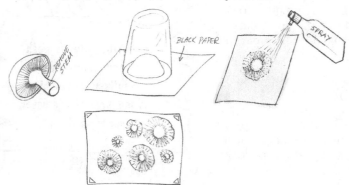

What's On a Twig?

You will need:

☐ **a magnifying glass**

Have a close look at a twig near the bottom of a broadleaf tree. In early spring or late fall you should be able to see the scars along the twig that were left when the leaves fell off.

You might be able to see a few black dots in the middle of the scars. These are the ends of veins that carried the food and water from the roots into the leaf.

In the spring you may be able to see new buds growing from the twig. These buds will eventually open and turn into new leaves as the weather gets warmer.

Look at a Tree's Ecosystem

Before you hike on, why not take a break? Sit very still and count the different animals and birds on one tree. Check for hollows big enough to hold a bird or squirrel's nest. Look for bugs — they nibble on the bark and leaves, and are in turn eaten by other creatures, such as birds.

Check for the mosses and lichens that grow on the tree trunk, too. They are also a part of the tree's ecosystem.

It's amazing how much life one tree can support. How many creatures can you identify and record in your nature notebook?

Learn to Identify Trees

With a little practice, you should be able to identify most of the common trees in your area. A good handbook is a valuable resource.

But what if you come across a tree that you don't recognize? Ask yourself these questions:

- Is it a conifer (evergreen) or a broadleaf tree?
- What is the tree's overall shape? Is it tall, round, does it appear "droopy"?
- What shape, color and size are the leaves or needles?
- Is there one leaf per twig, or several small leaflets?
- Depending on the season, what do the flowers, cones or fruit look like?
- What kind of bark does the tree have? Is it smooth, plated, shaggy or papery?
- If you're on a winter hike, what do the buds look like?

Answer these questions in your nature notebook. Take a bark rubbing and put a leaf in your plant press, too. When you get home, you can identify the tree. And next time, you'll be able to recognize it right away!

CONIFERS

CEDAR

PINE

FIR

74

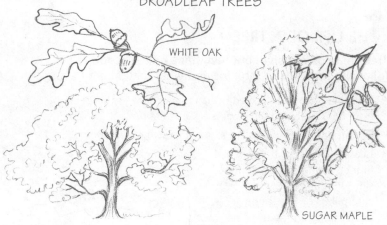

BROADLEAF TREES

WHITE OAK

SUGAR MAPLE

Tree Rubbings

This is a good way to make a collection of tree bark without having to actually strip it off the tree:

You will need:

☐ **dark colored crayon (paper peeled off) or charcoal**

☐ **a piece of lightweight paper (you could use a page of your nature notebook)**

- To get your rubbing, place the paper over the bark and rub the long side of the crayon over the paper.
- Try to hold the paper as still as possible (maybe a friend could hold the paper while you rub). See how many rubbings of different barks you can collect.

PINE BEECH HICKORY BIRCH CEDAR

THE LIFE OF A TREE

Trees may be massive, but they have enemies, too. The following are signs to look for and what they might mean:

- Tree bark that looks frayed or has marks on it — this could be from deer rubbing their antlers against the tree.
- Bright, barkless patches — signs of gnawing porcupines.
- Leaves with large holes or tunnels in them — these may be signs that insect larvae, caterpillars or beetles have been dining on them.
- Bumps on leaves — these could be signs that insects have been making their homes on these leaves. (This kind of insect home is called a gall.)
- Scars on the bark — these could be the result of fire.
- Torn off limbs or branches — perhaps the tree was hit by lightning. (Sometimes entire trees can be split in half!)
- Bark that is split and cracked — chances are that severe frost has damaged the tree. (To repair itself, a tree develops a scab-like covering over the crack.)
- Wood that has turned brittle or soft and spongy — this could happen when the tree receives too little light. (Clumped-together trees vie for light. The strongest trees survive, the weaker ones die.)

Did you know

that a big tree with lots of branches and leaves can drink 1,000 liters of water a day?

■

that you can estimate the age of a coniferous tree by counting the number of levels of branches from the bottom to the top of the tree? In general there will be one level of branches for each year the tree has been growing.

■

that you can tell (generally speaking) how old a tree is by the feel of its bark? A young tree has thin, smooth bark or skin while an older tree has thick, gnarled bark.

What's Dead but Lives On?

The tree may be dead but the log is teeming with life. If you come across a dead tree on a hike, take a few minutes to examine it close up. Try not to disturb its occupants.

After a Tree Dies

- The dead tree's soft wood and cracks make it easier for decomposers such as slugs and wood lice to move in, which in turn attracts centipedes and spiders that feed on them.
- Mosses and fungi grab hold of the bark.
- Other insects arrive and burrow into the wood.
- Bug-eating snakes and lizards then make their homes in, under, or near the log to take advantage of the good supply of food.
- Soon the log becomes its own mini-city with bugs building roads and tunnels through the wood.
- Birds and small animals chisel and scratch at the wood to get at the bugs inside.
- The log becomes so full of holes and the wood so soft that it crumbles into mulch. This mulch ends up as part of the forest soil. Other plants then use this soil to grow.

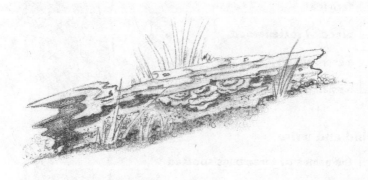

FOREST SCAVENGER HUNT

Everyone can play. Split into two groups. See how long it takes your group to find all (or most) of the items on the list. Make sure that no one gets lost. Keep your teammates in sight at all times.

Find the items mentioned on the list. If you make up your own list to suit the area you plan to hike, list some obvious "finds" (maple tree, ant hill, pine cone) along with harder ones (pop bottle, raccoon tracks).

Find:

☐ pine cone

☐ bird's feather

☐ maple tree leaf

☐ heart shaped leaf

☐ litter

☐ piece of spider web (store it in your nature notebook)

☐ weed seeds

☐ wild flower

☐ fern leaf

☐ piece of rotten wood

☐ mushroom

☐ a small piece of fallen birch bark

Find and write:

☐ the names of three bugs spotted

☐ the names of three birds spotted

Did you know

that prehistoric trees still exist?

The Wollemi pines, found in a tiny area of an Australian
rain forest, were believed to be extinct since the
Jurassic period, about 135 million years ago.
These huge pine trees (the biggest is about 40 meters
high) once covered vast areas of the world. When the
climate changed the trees began to disappear, remaining
only in this damp, protected gorge.

No one had any idea that these trees had survived. But
David Noble, a Parks and Wildlife Service officer,
noticed them when he was on a weekend hike in the area.
So far, only 39 trees have been counted, making them
one of the world's rarest plants.

Just imagine what treasures you might find
on your hike!

WETLANDS

THE WETLANDS HIKE

A wetlands hike can be tons of fun — thousands of animals, plants and bugs call the wetlands home. The sights, sounds and smells are unique.

You will need:

- [ ] **rubber boots**
- [ ] **long pants**
- [ ] **a hat (with netting over it if possible)**
- [ ] **insect repellent**
- [ ] **a pail**
- [ ] **a magnifying glass**
- [ ] **your nature notebook**
- [ ] **a pencil**
- [ ] **a hiking staff, if you have one**

Conservation

Hike around, not through, wetlands. Most protected areas have boardwalks or marked trails that allow you to go into the area. Wetlands are easily damaged by hikers.

What's so great about dragonflies? They feast on mosquitoes. One dragonfly can gobble dozens and dozens of the pesky mosquitoes a day. Look for dragonflies when hiking around the wetlands. If you don't see any, the marsh may be in environmental trouble. Dragonflies are often the first victims of pollution.

HELPFUL HINT:
Consider carefully before taking your dog on a hike. Dogs will scare off wildlife and chances are you'll spend a lot of time yelling for the dog to "heel." If you must take the dog with you, tie a little bell around its neck. Not only will you hear it but so will other animals. Don't forget the leash.

Did you know

that wetlands are also called bogs, fens, swamps, marshes, bayous, muskegs, quagmires, sloughs (pronounced "slooz") and potholes?

Types of Wetlands

There are four basic types of wetlands:

Marshes are usually found near or beside large water sources. The water may measure between 15 cm and 2 m deep. Marsh plants, such as cattails and bulrushes, are soft-stemmed. You'll also find lily pads and lots of underwater plants in marshes.

Swamps are wooded areas that are filled with water during spring.

Bogs are formed over deep depressions left by glaciers. They are usually made of peat, a combination of mosses and other decomposed plants. There is no drainage for water so the ground is always mushy. They support very little animal or plant life. Whatever you do, don't walk on a bog.

Fens are also made of peat. They have some drainage for water so there is varied animal and plant life.

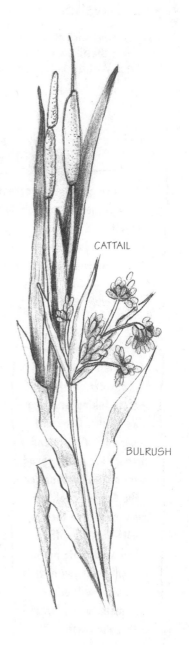

CATTAIL

BULRUSH

Make an Underwater Viewer

Take a peek at plant and fish life by making a viewer.

You will need:

☐ **a milk carton**

☐ **a plastic bag or plastic wrap**

☐ **an elastic band**

☐ **a friend or adult to accompany you**

- Cut the milk carton in half and cut the bottom out of the carton.
- Stretch the plastic over the bottom of the carton. Secure the plastic with the elastic band.

Ask a friend or adult to accompany you to the water's edge. Lower the viewer into the water, making sure water does not slosh over the top, and take a peek. You'll have to put your face right into the carton.

Wetlands Bugs

The wetlands are home to lots of bugs. Many of them live in, on or lay eggs in the water. Scoop up a bug with your pail and have a close look. Careful — some nip. Record your finds in your notebook. Here are some common wetlands bugs:

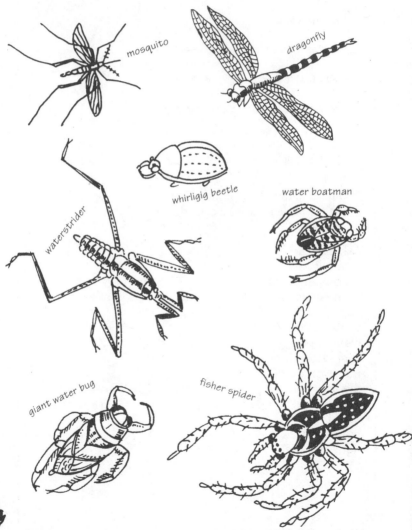

mosquito

dragonfly

whirligig beetle

water boatman

waterstrider

giant water bug

fisher spider

Wetlands Creatures

Can you spot these wetlands creatures?

duck

heron

bat

frog

salamander

muskrat

toad

snake

leech

turtle

Wetlands Plants

The wetlands support lots of plants, many quite different from those found anywhere else. Here are some wetlands plants you may see on your hike:

Arrowhead: is sometimes called "duck potato" because ducks like the potato-shaped tubers that grow as big as rubber balls. It has three-petal white flowers and leaves shaped like arrowheads.

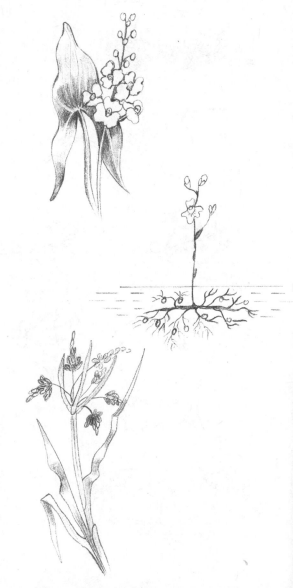

Bladderwort: is a meat-eating plant that has no roots but floats on, and just under, the surface of the water.

Bulrushes: have triangular or round stems with small brownish flowers at the top.

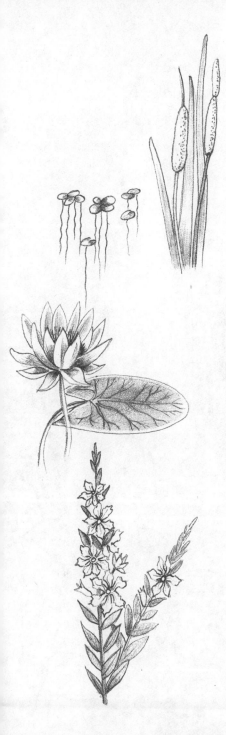

Cattails: shaped like brown cigars, they stand tall all year round and release thousands of white snowflake-like seeds in the fall.

Duckweed: a rootless, flowering plant that floats on top of the water. It is a food source for birds and insects.

Water lilies: have floating leaves and a flowering plant, attached to long, underwater stems.

Purple loosestrife: sometimes called "beautiful killers," these long-stemmed plants sprout small, purple flowers. Purple loosestrife is not a native North American plant and has no natural enemies. It is now taking over our wetlands and choking out other plants like bulrushes and cattails.

BEACH

THE BEACH HIKE

You will need:

- [ ] water shoes or running shoes (sharp objects hide in the sand)

- [ ] sunscreen
- [ ] a bucket
- [ ] your nature notebook
- [ ] a pencil
- [ ] a plastic bag
- [ ] drinking water

What a great feeling to stand beside the water's edge and see a vast expanse of blue. Oceans, seas and great lakes have always evoked strong feelings in people.

And yet our lakes, rivers and oceans are singing the blues. Pollution is killing off entire species. But there are a few things we, as beach hikers, can do:

We can *stop* removing huge amounts of material from the water's edge. Collecting shells from the beach is fun, but cast-off shells have a role to play in the ecology of the ocean. Most of these treasures are found around the drift line — the line left by high tide (also called strand line or tide line). If you want to collect *a few* mementos, hit the beach before the gulls and birds do — just after high tide.

Why not carry a bag with you and pick up any garbage you see? Nylon fishing lines and plastic six-pack holders cause all sorts of trouble for birds. Bottle caps, glass — all people pollution should be picked up carefully and discarded properly. The exceptions: never touch a used hypodermic needle or an old oil drum. Tell the police.

There it is — a deserted beach. Why not take the plunge? Hang on, there's probably a reason why the beach is deserted. Tides could pull you out to sea, whirlpools could drag you under or the water could be polluted. **BEFORE YOU SWIM** — know the area, obey posted signs and make sure an adult has given you the okay. And, of course, never swim alone.

Tide

Tides are caused by the gravitational pull of the moon, and to some extent the sun. Look for signs of high and low tide. Look for the strand line along the beach and chances are you'll find lots of sea treasures. Coastlines have two high tides and two low tides every 24 hours.

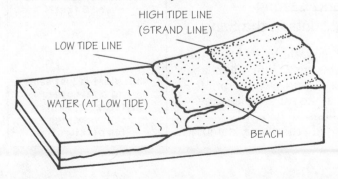

HIGH TIDE LINE (STRAND LINE)

LOW TIDE LINE

WATER (AT LOW TIDE)

BEACH

Waves wear away the coastline. Small rocks, shells and ocean debris are slapped against the coast and cliffs. The wind that pushes the waves also tears away rocks and sand. Notice the layers of rock. Check to see if you can spot any birds' nests. Unless accompanied by an adult, stay away from cliffs and arches. Even if you have an adult with you, be careful walking along the top of the cliff. Not only could the land give way and send you crashing down the cliff but you could stumble upon a blowhole — caused by waves pushing from below.

Do not explore caves and hollows in rocks during low tide without an adult and without knowing when high tide is expected. It's possible to become trapped in the cave by a high tide.

Sand

If you like collecting rocks, why not try making a sand collection too? Sand comes in all different colors and textures. You can keep your sand collection in little bottles — film canisters or old, washed-out pill bottles are great.

Sand Casting — Footprints in the Sand

Making plaster casts of animal tracks is easy. Why not make a cast of your own footprints right in the sand? Follow the directions on page 43. Choose hard, slightly damp,

Did you know

that the Mediterranean Sea hardly has a tide at all while the difference in high and low tide in The Bay of Fundy in New Brunswick can be over 50 feet?

■

that glass is just sand and a few other ingredients, heated to a very high temperature?

flat sand to make your foot imprint. Let the plaster sit for a few hours — why not hike on and pick it up on the way back?

Sea Shell Sculptures

- Make a hollow in the sand.
- Arrange shells in the hollow.
- Mix plaster of paris and pour in.
- Let set for 15 to 30 minutes.
- Wrap in paper or plastic and take home.
- Let set for a few days.

Sea Birds

Beach and sea birds have adapted to life beside the water. The bills on sea birds are designed to spear or scoop. Their feet are webbed or designed to scoot across the sand. Many sea birds gobble fish, others munch on shelled creatures. Watch closely and you may see a

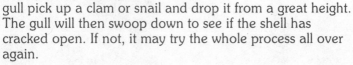

gull pick up a clam or snail and drop it from a great height. The gull will then swoop down to see if the shell has cracked open. If not, it may try the whole process all over again.

Keep an eye out for the following birds: the herring gull (it has a red dot on its bill); herons (the great blue heron is probably as tall as you are!); and sanderlings (small sand-colored birds that run up and down the beach in search of food).

Tide Pools and Pool Dipping

You will need:

☐ **a net**

☐ **a jar**

Find a pool or small inlet along the water's edge and do a little dipping.

On the surface you might find beetles, mosquito larvae and bugs zipping across the surface like skaters on ice.

Look again and see crabs crawling along the bottom, starfish in wait for lunch and fish on the hunt. Snails may be found creeping across a mossy rock, on the underside of damp leaves or hanging onto the stems of plants.

Dip the net in and see what you catch.

Put the creatures in your jar along with damp leaves. Watch how the creatures react. Let them go before your hike resumes.

BEACH SCAVENGER HUNT

Everyone can play. Split into two groups. See how long it takes your group to find all (or most of) the items on the list. Make sure that no one gets lost. Keep your teammates in sight at all times.

Find the items mentioned on the list. If you make up your own list to suit the area you plan to hike, list some obvious "finds" along with more difficult ones. You can make it as easy or as hard as you like!

Find:

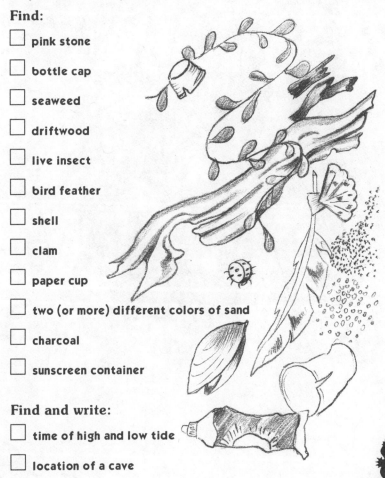

☐ pink stone

☐ bottle cap

☐ seaweed

☐ driftwood

☐ live insect

☐ bird feather

☐ shell

☐ clam

☐ paper cup

☐ two (or more) different colors of sand

☐ charcoal

☐ sunscreen container

Find and write:

☐ time of high and low tide

☐ location of a cave

WINTER

THE WINTER HIKE

 Unless you live in a warm climate, winter hiking is not usually hiking at all but snowshoeing or cross-country skiing. But don't let that stop you! You might think there is nothing to see in the winter — but you'd be wrong. In fact, there can be *more* to see. Everything changes according to the seasons. Try to hike the same trail once a season. The changes in birds, plants and animals are astonishing.

 Dress smart, in layers (cotton or wool on the inside). Don't forget hats, gloves, and scarves. And yes, sunscreen and sunglasses (or snow goggles) too!

Wildlife

 Once the leaves have fallen from the trees, you can see nests in the branches. Animals can be easier to spot without dense undergrowth. Look for animal tracks in the snow. Even though some mammals hibernate, and many birds migrate south for the winter, there's still plenty to see!

Tree Identification

 Coniferous trees look about the same in the snow. Broadleaf trees can be identified by their shape. You can also look at the buds on the branches. These buds contain the beginnings of the next year's leaves, flowers and twigs. Different trees have different types of buds.

Make a Permanent Impression of a Snowflake

You will need:

☐ **a small pane of glass**

☐ **hairspray**

- Spray the glass with hairspray and store it in the freezer.
- When it snows, take the pane of glass outdoors and catch snowflakes on it.
- When you have collected enough flakes, take the glass back indoors and leave it at room temperature for 15 minutes.

The snowflakes will melt and evaporate, but the impressions of their intricate and delicate patterns will remain. Can you find two alike?

Search for Snow Fleas

You will need:

☐ **a magnifying glass**

On warm and sunny winter days, check the south side of a tree near the ground. You may see what looks like pepper on the ground. Have a closer look with your magnifying glass. The little speckles are in fact tiny insects called snow fleas. They use their little tails like springs to bounce into the air.

Make a Pair of Snow Goggles

The winter sun is very bright because it reflects off the white snow as well as shining down from above. A pair of snow goggles helps cut down the sun's glare and makes things a little easier on your eyes. Here's how to make a pair of your own.

You will need:

☐ a sheet of construction paper (preferably black)

☐ scissors

☐ elastic or string

- Cut out an ordinary mask, like the ones used around Halloween, from the paper.
- Instead of cutting holes for the eyes, cut a few narrow slits. These slits will protect your eyes from the glare but you will still be able to see where you are going.

Instead of paper you might try cutting two of the egg holders from an egg carton. Cut slits in the bottoms and attach with string or elastic.

Science in a backpack

Make a Cast of an Animal Track in Winter

If you hike during the winter you can still collect animal tracks. Follow the directions for making a cast (see page 43). You will need all the items for making a warm weather cast, *plus* a a water sprayer/mister.

Spray a light film of water over the track and let it freeze for a minute or two. This will create a nice smooth and hard surface on which the plaster can set.

It's best to go searching for winter tracks when the temperature is quite cold and the snow is hard. Once the plaster has set you can dig it up, wrap it up and take it home. Let it harden for a few hours before handling it.

Frostbite and Hypothermia

There are two important dangers to be aware of when winter hiking — frostbite and hypothermia (low body temperature). Be sure to stay dry and keep bundled up, no matter how silly you may look! Keep an eye on your buddies too, and head back *right away* if you notice any of these signs in yourself or others:

Frostbite

- numbness in fingers, toes, face or ears
- pale or greyish-yellow skin

Hypothermia

- shivering
- slurred speech and clumsiness
- stumbling
- drowsiness

CITY

THE CITY HIKE

A hike through a city or town — sounds like fun! Let's start with a bare-bones look at the inner-city hike.

You will need:

- [ ] **a water container (you may not be able to get a drink unless you pay for it)**
- [ ] **sunscreen**
- [ ] **a hat**
- [ ] **money (small change, cab fare, bus tickets)**
- [ ] **a street map**
- [ ] **identification and health card**

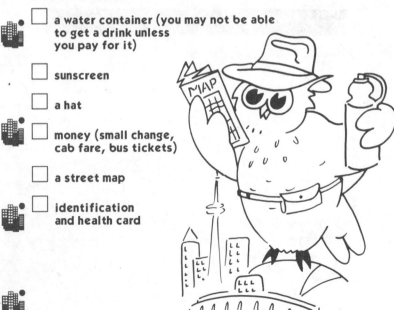

Street Smarts

You can get lost in the city but there are enough resources around to get you un-lost in a hurry. The dangers of the city hike are different from the dangers of a forest or beach hike, but the same rules apply. For example, always tell an adult where you're going and what time you'll be back. Brush up on your street smarts. Here's a brief list of Do's and Don'ts to refresh your memory:

- Don't head out on your own. Always hike in groups. And, as always, try to bring an adult along.
- If someone you don't know talks to you, walk away. It's okay to ask a stranger for help, but never go any anywhere with someone you don't know.
- Do ask a police officer, cab or bus driver or a parent with small children for directions if you're lost.
- Do discuss a lost and found plan before you set out.
- Do watch for traffic.
- Don't feed or try to befriend any animals you may encounter, including innocent-looking stray dogs.

City Wildlife

Animals are everywhere — rabbits and raccoons in parks or backyards, squirrels in trees or under rafters, rats in the alleys, pigeons in town squares, skunks in gulleys, ducks in ponds, even falcons on roof tops. Animals are trying, some very successfully, to adapt to city life.

Don't approach any of these animals and never offer them food.

Raccoons: Raccoons can eat just about anything — you name it. Look for raccoons in sewers, garages, attics, culverts, a building's ventilation system, and yes, also in trees.

Rats: They have been called the animal that has most successfully adapted to urban life. But as a hiker you need not worry, since rats are nocturnal animals (they prefer to sleep during the day and come out at night), move very fast and don't like human company.

Squirrels: They're so common, so much a part of the scenery, it's easy to take the sight of them for granted. Squirrels are intelligent — watch how they store their nuts in places close to their nests. Squirrels are cooperative — one squirrel will knock down nuts from a tree while a group of them shares the falling booty. They are also relatively harmless.

People: True, people don't really qualify as "wild" life — but people are interesting to watch. Just as you might take time out on a forest hike to watch a bird or smell a daisy, why not stop for a moment and watch the people go by? Park yourself on a bench and just watch. You'll be surprised at how much fun it is!

City Birds

Pigeons: Most people aren't too crazy about these messy city dwellers. Pigeons have had a relationship with people for thousands of years. They were once raised as food — bred for the pot.

Starlings: Starlings are not native to North America. They were originally imported from England, but hundreds of millions now live in the U.S. and Canada.

A word of warning — don't try to take any animal home. This rule stands for city or forest hikes. Trying to save a wild animal is very difficult. Wild animals often die in captivity. The rare ones that recover cannot readapt to life in the wild. If you know that an animal is in severe pain, leave it alone and contact the Humane Society.

City Plants

When you're walking down the city street, stop for a second. Do you see the dandelion struggling to grow in the cracks of cement? What about the pigweed, knotweeds or flowers — seeds set loose from home flowerpots — that decorate the streets? These plants are often called "crack-dwellers" — plants determined to grow with minimal light, water and clean air. They're stubborn and hardy.

Urban Architecture

Look up . . . look way up. Amazing, isn't it? Most of us could walk down the same street for years and years and never look up past the first floor of a building. But there is a difference between walking and hiking down a street. The object of walking is to get somewhere, the goal of hiking is to exercise (naturally) and learn through the journey. So look up at the architecture!

Architecture is the science and art of building. Look carefully around you. You'll find lots of variation in building styles in different cities and towns, and even in different parts of the same town.

What are the buildings you see made of: wood, brick, stone, cement, glass? Do the materials used to make the buildings around you say something about the surrounding area: nearby forests, brickworks, quarries? What about climate?

Some style clues to look for are:

- shapes of windows
- types of roof
- pillars
- height of a structure

Sketch various styles in your notebook, then head for the library to see if you can identify them.

Did you know

that parks are a relatively new invention? Years ago, when city people wanted to go for a walk they often strolled through the cemetery.

A Cemetery Trek

A jaunt through a cemetery can tell you a great deal about the history of the city. Most cemeteries are divided up by religion. Notice the wording on the tombstones. Very old gravestones, or pioneer burying grounds, may not even list the names of small children who are buried there, so common was the death of babies and toddlers in the not-so-distant past.

Notice the common first names of times past. Run your fingers over the lettering and see if you can read the epitaphs. See if you can make out common dates of death. In some communities half the population might have been wiped out at one time by a disease such as smallpox.

Many cemeteries also have a vast array of tree and plant life, some with identifying labels — another interesting way to learn about a city.

When Was It Built?

When was this road built? Check the sewer lids. Many will have dates on them. How old is this building? Look at the cornerstones of buildings: they too may be dated. Once we might have dated a road by the style of lamp posts but many designers now use fake antique posts so they are not reliable indicators.

Food

You're probably starving by now. Well, you're in the right place. As you've probably noticed, most established cities have ethnic areas. One of the easiest ways to learn about a new culture is through its food. Try something that you've never tasted before. Go on — be brave! But if you're not, you're sure to find your old favorites here too.

CITY SCAVENGER HUNT

Everyone can play. Split into two groups. See how long it takes your group to find all (or most of) the items on the list. Make sure that no one gets lost. Keep your teammates in sight at all times.

Find the items mentioned on the list or mark down the place and time spotted. If you make up your own list to suit the area you plan to hike, list some obvious "finds" along with more difficult ones. You can make it as easy or as hard as you like!

Find:

☐ travel brochures

☐ business card from a store

☐ free newspaper

☐ real estate listing for houses

☐ postcard

☐ flyer for pizza delivery

☐ napkin

☐ subway or bus schedule

☐ a safety brochure
(hint: try the police station)

☐ gum wrapper

☐ toilet paper square

Find and write:

 ☐ the cross streets of a pay phone

☐ the address of a house with a fire hydrant in front

☐ the address of two Block Parents (Canada) or Safe Homes (U.S.)

☐ the name of a street that begins with your first initial

☐ the date on the cornerstone of the town hall

☐ the streets that border a park

THE ARMCHAIR HIKER

Can't get outside today? In addition to the "rainy day activities" we've included throughout the book, here are some things for you to do at home to help improve your hiking skills and keep you in that "Take a Hike" frame of mind.

Choose the correct answer. Give yourself five points for every question answered correctly. The answers are below, and some have a page number beside them. If you don't understand the answer, flip to the page and read all about it!

1 You're in the woods. It's an hour before nightfall. You've lost your friends and haven't the faintest idea where you are. But you have a compass, a map, warm clothes and even an apple. What should you do?

a Close your eyes and point in a direction. Walk in that direction. You're bound to end up somewhere!

b Hug a tree.

c Sit down and cry.

2 It's a beautiful summer day. A friend stops by and wants to go for a hike. You can't reach your mom and dad but you hike all the time, know the area well, and besides, your mom gave you permission to go hiking with a different friend last week. Should you go?

a Yes, but just for a little while, and if you leave a note.

b Yes, your mom and dad wouldn't want you to miss a golden hiking opportunity.

c No, not without your parents' knowledge.

3 You're on a beach hike and spot a neat cave on the water's edge. You have chalk to mark the way in, and therefore find your way out, and it is low tide. Should you go exploring?

a Sure, what could happen?

b Yes, but make sure it's an hour after you've eaten.

c No, too risky.

4 You're on the trail and it's cold and damp. Your partner is not dressed very warmly and is shivering. Should you head home?

a Yes, right away.

b Yes, as soon as you spot five more species of birds.

c Nah, your friend will probably be fine once he/she gets going.

5 You come across a small bear cub playing. Your little brother wants to play with it. After all, he says, it's too small to be able to hurt anybody. Should you stop him?

a   Yes, right away.

b   What for? It's such a cute little furry bundle!

c   Only if you spot the mother nearby.

1) Answer: B) Hug-A-Tree — that means, set up camp and prepare for the night. Page 23. (Crying is okay too, for a little while.)

2) Answer: C) No. Hiking is serious stuff. Kids or adults should never hike anywhere without someone at home knowing the route, the time of return and so on. This is not a kid rule — this is a people rule. Page 4.

3) Answer: C) Probably not. When is high tide? Is there a knowledgeable adult with you? And chalk washes away easily. As a marker into and out of a watery cave it's not very reliable. Page 94.

4) Answer: A) Yes, your friend needs to get warm. Wrap him/her as warmly as possible and head for the nearest warm place immediately. Read up on hypothermia in your first aid book. Page 103.

5) Answer: A) Yes! You can be sure that mother bear is somewhere nearby (even if you can't see her). While your little brother might be just playing, she will think he's attacking her baby — and she'll get pretty mean. Pages 40-41.

If your score was:

0 . . . Hey, you were supposed to read the book *first!*
5 . . . Tenderfoot.
10 . . You're still green, but you've got potential!
15 . . A great hiking buddy.
20 . . Experienced hiker.
25 . . Why are you sitting there? Hit the trail!

KNOW YOUR KNOTS

When you're out hiking, you will find it handy to know several basic knots. You can also use these knots in other outdoor activities, like camping, boating or fishing. Try these knots at home, before you set out on your hike. And don't get discouraged — practice makes perfect!

First, the basics: the end of the rope that is being tied is called the "working end." The other end is called the "standing end." The part between is called the "bight." In an overhand loop, the working end crosses over the standing end. In an underhand loop, the working end crosses behind the standing end.

Overhand Knot

The simplest knot to tie is an overhand knot (also known as a "thumb knot.") You'll recognize this knot as the one used to keep the thread from slipping through the eye of a sewing needle. It can be used to make a rope easier to hold onto. The overhand knot is difficult to untie when wet or when using thin rope.

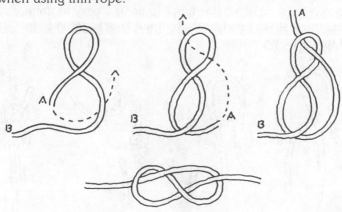

Bowline

The bowline is one of the oldest and most useful knots to know. It is very secure and won't slip under strain (mountain climbers use it to tie their ropes around their waists). Use a bowline when you want to make a loop that will not slip. It is quick and easy to untie. You can also use the bowline to attach a rope to an object for hoisting, such as suspending your pack from a tree while hiking. You could also make a temporary leash for your dog with a bowline. Don't use this knot on very stiff or slippery rope.

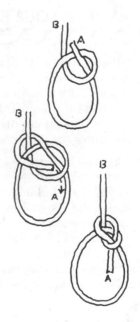

Sheet Bend

The sheet bend is very useful for tying two ropes of different thicknesses together so that they won't slip apart, or for joining a rope to a loop. The sheet bend is also called a "flag bend" when it is used to join the corners of a flag to a hoisting rope. It is quick to tie and easy to untie. Don't use a sheet bend, though, if the knot is going to be put under heavy strain.

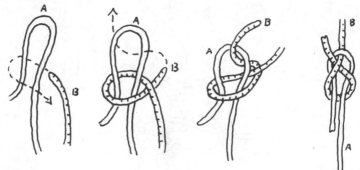

Clove Hitch

A clove hitch is the knot to use when tying a rope to a pole. It is also used by sailors to moor their boats (since it can be tied with one hand, sailors can moor their boats while holding a railing with the other). It can slip with motion, though, so only use it temporarily. (You wouldn't want to use it to tie your dog to a post, for example.) You'll probably want to use clove hitches to secure ropes to tent poles or when making a lean-to.

Slip Knot

Also known as the "timber hitch," this knot is often used to drag, pull, raise or lower objects. It is easy to tie and is very secure, no matter how heavy the load. It also comes apart easily.

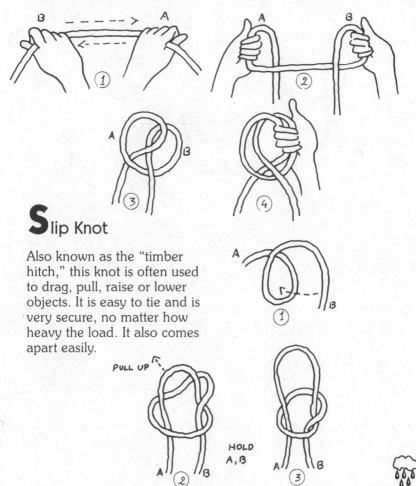

Reef Knot

The reef knot (or "square knot") has been used by sailors
for centuries to tie two ropes of equal size together. We now
use it for things like tying together a broken shoe lace or for
tying up packages. It lies flat so it is also good for tying
bandages or for other situations when the knot must hang
over a shoulder or next to the skin. Don't use a reef knot to
join two different-sized ropes as it will not hold well under
strain.

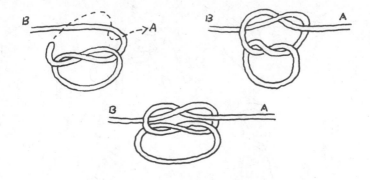

Choose the best answer:

You're setting out for your first hike of the year. Just as you're tying up your hiking boots, one of the laces breaks. You quickly repair it with

   a an overhand knot

   b a reef knot

   c a sheet bend

   d a clove hitch

2

You decide to do some underwater viewing on your hike but you don't want to carry your heavy pack with you to the water's edge. Because you don't want animals getting into your lunch, you use this knot to sling it up into a tree.

   a an overhand knot

   b a sheet bend

   c a clove hitch

   d a bowline knot

   e a slip knot

3 You're at the top of a steep hill, your friend is at the bottom. He doesn't think he can climb it. You throw him a line with these tied at regular intervals, so that he can hang on to it and make it up the hill.

a overhand knots

b reef knots

c clove hitches

d bowline knots

e slip knots

4 It looks like rain. You and your friends make a temporary shelter using

a a reef knot

b a sheet bend

c a clove hitch

d a bowline knot

e a slip knot

to attach a space blanket to a branch.

5 But one of the corners of your space blanket already has a rope attached to it. You secure this corner with

a an overhand knot

b a reef knot

c a sheet bend

d a clove hitch

e a slip knot

6 You need something to sit on in your shelter since the ground is really damp. There's an old log down the trail that would be perfect. But how are you going to drag it all the way to your camp? You decide to attach a piece of rope to it using

a   a reef knot

b   a sheet bend

c   a clove hitch

d   a bowline knot

e   a slip knot

7 While helping to get the huge log into position, one of your friends scrapes his hand. You make a temporary bandage for him using

a   an overhand knot

b   a reef knot

c   a sheet bend

d   a clove hitch

e   a bowline knot

ANSWERS

1 b) a reef knot
2 e) a bowline knot
3 a) overhand knots
4 b) a sheet bend
5 d) a clove hitch
6 e) a slip knot
7 b) a reef knot

125

HIKERS IN HISTORY

Many of history's great explorers had to travel over vast areas of land, sea or ice to make their discoveries. Of course, most of them didn't walk *all* the way, but all of them had to do quite a bit of hiking on their travels. Match these famous hikers with the descriptions of their "hikes" described below.

a   **Rick Hansen**

b   **David Livingston**

c   **John Chapman**
     (a.k.a. Johnny Appleseed)

d   **Paleo-Indians**

e   **David Thompson**

f   **Neil Armstrong**

g   **Roald Amundsen**

h   **Marco Polo**

 i   **Laura Secord**

1 My people and I were the first to discover what we now call North America. We hiked from Asia, across the Bering Strait (it was dry land at the time), and down into America. The hike took many, many generations. We settled most of North and South America. Who are we?

2 When I left Italy in 1272 A.D. I was 15 years old. I went from Italy to what is now Israel and hiked through Iraq and Iran (then Persia) along the southern part of Russia to China. Eventually I went to Southeast Asia, India, Persia, Turkey and Greece. No one would have heard of my great hikes had I not been captured as a prisoner of war later in my life. I dictated the details of my great hike to a fellow prisoner. Who am I?

3 I was the adventurer who from about 1790 to 1826 explored, surveyed and mapped central North America. Some say I covered more than 80,000 kilometers of territory. Accurate maps were made because of my observations. Two of my main contributions were the exploration and mapping of the headwaters of the Mississippi and the entire coast of Lake Superior. Who am I?

4 My hike helped win a battle. During the War of 1812 between the United States and Britain, the British colonies of Upper and Lower Canada were attacked. I overheard American officers planning a surprise attack, and walked 30 kilometers from Queenston to Beaver Dams to warn the officers there. Who am I?

5 From 1852 onward I hiked through the southern third of the African Continent. I crossed the Kalahari Desert, ventured northwest to Luanda, and went across the continent to Quelimane. I became the first European to cross the continent. In 1871 at a place called Ujiji on Lake Tanganyika I became very ill. An American journalist, Henry Stanley, a pretty good hiker himself, found me (although to my knowledge I was never lost!). Who am I?

6 My most famous hike was a chilly one. I hoped to be the first person to reach the South Pole in Antarctica. My companions and I began our hike to the pole on October 20, 1911. On December 14, after hiking nearly 1,400 kilometers, we reached the South Pole. We stayed there for three days making astronomical observations before returning safely home. Who am I?

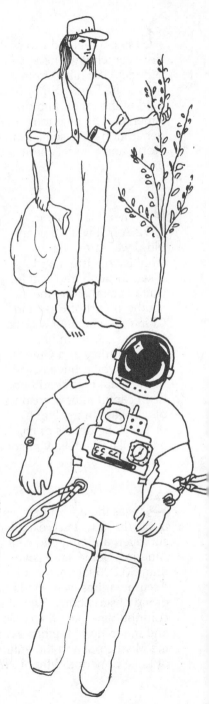

7 I took one small step for man, but a giant leap for mankind. Who am I?

8 In the early 1800s I hiked through Pennsylvania, Ohio, Indiana, and Illinois. I carried with me a large bag of seeds for the settlers to plant. Sometimes I traded the seeds for food but if the people were too poor I would just give them seeds. Who am I?

9 It began in Vancouver in 1985. My hike-on-wheels took me to 34 different countries. My goal was to cover about 40,000 km, a distance equivalent to travelling around the world. My hike was called the "Man in Motion" tour and was done, in part, to increase public awareness and support for the physically disabled. My "hike" raised $20 million for spinal cord research and wheelchair sports. Who am I?

1. d) Paleo-Indians (the ancestors of all North and South American Indians)

2. h) Marco Polo

3. e) David Thompson

4. i) Laura Secord

5. b) David Livingston

6. g) Roald Amundsen

7. f) Neil Armstrong (the first person to walk on the moon)

8. c) John Chapman

9. a) Rick Hansen

Books to CHECK OUT

Hit the library, then the bookstore.You'll probably want copies of some books for your own, since you'll be referring to them often.

Here's a list of useful titles to start you off.

The Bird Book, by Neil and Karen Dawe. Workman Publishing, 1988

Birdwise, by Pamela M. Hickman. Kids Can Press, 1988

Born Smart? Why Animals Do What They Do, by Peter Cook and Laura Suzuki. Scholastic Canada, 1993

Bugwise, by Pamela Hickman. Kids Can Press, 1990

Earthcycles and Ecosystems, by Beth Savan. Kids Can Press, 1991

Experiment with Weather, by Miranda Bower. Scholastic Canada, 1992

Introducing Birds, by Pamela Hickman. Pembroke Publishers, 1992

Introducing Trees, by Pamela Hickman. Pembroke Publishers, 1992

The Kids Cottage Book, by Jane Drake and Ann Love. Kids Can Press, 1993

The Kid's Nature Book, by Susan Milford. Williamson Publishing Co., 1989

Leaf and Tree Guide, by Rona Beame. Workman Publishing, 1989

Life in the Woods, by Rosanne Hooper. Scholastic Canada, 1993

Maps and Mapping, by Barbara Taylor. Kingfisher Books, 1993

 Plantwise, by Pamela M. Hickman. Kids Can Press, 1991

Spotter's Guide to Animals, Tracks and Signs, by Alfred Leutscher. Usborne Publishing, 1985

Spotter's Guide to Birds of North America, by Dr. Philip Burton. Usborne Publishing, 1991

Spotter's Guide to Trees of North America, by Alan Mitchell. Mayflower Books Inc., 1992

Spotter's Guide to Wildflowers of North America, by Michael A. Ruggiero. Mayflower Books Inc., 1992

Take a Hike, the Sierra Club Kid's Guide to Hiking and Backpacking, by Lynn Foster. Little Brown and Company, 1991

Wetlands, by Pamela M. Hickman. Kids Can Press, 1993

The Wildflower Field Guide (and Press), by Carol Ann Campbell. Somerville House Publishing, 1993.

For More Information

If you would like to get more information on the Hug-A-Tree program described on page 23, please contact Hug-A-Tree at 6465 Lance Way, San Diego, CA, USA 92120, Phone (619) 286-7536.

INDEX

THE AUTHORS

Sharon McKay is a writer, editor, broadcaster and the author of several books, including *The Picky Eater, The New Child Safety Handbook,* and *Streetproofing Gently and Creatively.*

David MacLeod is a businessman, Cub leader and avid hiker. He is co-author (with his son) of a multi-media column in *City Parent* newsmagazine.

Together, **Sharon and David** are husband and wife and the authors of three other popular books for kids: *Chalk Around the Block, The Halloween Book,* and *Kick the Can.* They live in a log house in Kilbride, Ontario, with their two sons, Sam and Joe.